A Little Bit of Heaven on Rural Route Two

By: Angela Kanady Slay

"A Little Bit of Heaven on Rural Route Two" is dedicated to the very ones who were the real-life inspiration for the book. My parents, J.R. Kanady and Frances Annette Greene Kanady, my sisters Laura Jaye Kanady Cormier and Charlotte Annette Kanady Smith.

Family is everything. For those that cannot see it, my hope and prayer for you is that you put aside differences and reconnect with your family, not wasting another valuable moment you could be living with love instead of the regrets you will one day have.

Love hard, live fully.

Chapter 1

Aliza Rae lay on her back on the "soft grass". That's what she, her sisters and her cousins called it. The bright green, wispy grass that grew just in this patch on the creekbank, but nowhere else in Pa's pasture, was a wonderful place for a picnic, a nap or just daydreaming like Aliza Rae was doing now. She was seven years old, and she was trying to remember her very first memory. She guessed she was probably around four. She remembered sitting on Mama's lap, her head against Mama's chest and her face toward the mountain in view right outside the windows. As Mama hummed a lullaby, Aliza Rae could hear Mama's every heartbeat in her ear. Outside, the mountain appeared to sway with each movement of Mama's rocking chair and the wood floor creaked softly.

Looking back, Aliza Rae realized that was her first real memory of home, love and family, but it would be many years before she realized what a rare and priceless gift their parents had given them. She got up, wiped the dirt off the seat of her shorts and walked back home.

The little white house at the bottom of the hill of that old dirt road had always been home. Mama and Daddy had met at the small local college in a small town called Cleveland, Georgia. They married on a regular old weekday in an old country store. The store owner was the preacher, and their witnesses were the preacher's wife and the bread delivery man. Their life together started simply and without fanfare. They just quietly became Mr. and Mrs. Jake and Sissy Hubbard for the rest of their lives. They lived with Jake's parents and sister while they built the little white house down the hill from Pa and Granny. It was made from wood from an old church that had been torn down and, years later if you looked closely, you could still see the name of a girl who went to the church still etched in the wood. That same girl would go on to teach the three girls in elementary school.

The house was finished when the oldest Hubbard daughter, Laurel Jayne, was just a tiny baby. Two years later, Carley Anne was born, and Aliza Rae came along three years after that. Her baby book held the entry of Jake's first impression of her, which said "she looks just like the other two." Years later, Aliza Rae would realize that her daddy, like most men, had probably wanted to add a boy to the family. He and Mama had even gone through the preliminary steps of adopting. When Mama found out she was pregnant again, they withdrew their application. When Mama miscarried, they saw it as God telling them their family was complete. Jake didn't get his boy, but he did get the next closest thing in the tomboy that was Aliza Rae. She was his constant companion to the barn, fishing or anywhere else that he went. She loved when Daddy would head out the door and ask if she wanted to go with him and she never refused. She loved spending time with her daddy, whether it was sitting quietly on a creekbank or going to pick up cow and pig feed at the Farmers Exchange. Aliza Rae loved to follow Daddy around in the store taking in the sights of farm equipment and seeds and then, once the big bags of feed were thrown from the loading dock onto the back of Daddy's truck, she loved to jump from the loading dock onto the bags of feed.

The Hubbards lived very happy lives in that little white house. Mama and Daddy believed in being grateful for what they had, sharing extra any time they had it, and, most importantly, keeping God at the center of their lives. The girls never wanted for anything. They didn't realize they might not have as much as others because their parents never approached life that way. They lived simply, creating happy, lifelong memories with friends and family along the way. They belonged to a little country church a couple miles from home and there was never a time their girls had to ask if they were going to church. If the doors were open, they were going. Life for the Hubbards and most other nearby families centered around Shoal Creek Baptist Church.

The little white house at the end of the dirt road was filled with love and happiness, but not without the occasional drama that comes from having three girls share a double bed, a bedroom and a bathroom.

Chapter 2

"Mama! Aliza Rae wet the bed again!" yelled Laurel Jayne, waking up the whole house. Aliza Rae was in the middle of a dream and was halted awake. Why did Laurel Jayne have to be such a tattletale? Well, if she told herself the truth, Aliza Rae would have to admit it wasn't like she could've hid it anyway since the three girls shared a double bed. Her sisters always made her sleep in the middle, telling her they were protecting her since any monsters lurking under the bed would grab them both first. They hated it if she climbed over them or pulled the covers off in the middle of the night. And Aliza Rae hated to pad across the cold wooden floor in the dark to get to the bathroom anyway, so she guessed in her sleep she thought she went but then wet the bed.

At five years old, she knew she shouldn't still be wetting the bed, but it served Laurel Jayne and Carley Anne right for being so mean to her anyway! Mama sleepily walked into the room and told the girls it was nearly time to get up anyway, so to go ahead and get a quick bath while she changed the sheets. Laurel Jayne and Carley Anne fussed about having to get a bath in the cold bathroom so early in the morning, but Mama never fussed at Aliza Rae about the wet sheets and just went about the business of putting them in the washing machine, putting on clean sheets and then heading to the kitchen to fix breakfast. Aliza Rae thought her mama was the prettiest, kindest mama ever and she wanted to be just like her when she grew up. But there was no time to think about that now. Today was sale barn day!

Aliza Rae jumped up and ran to the bathroom to wash off and get dressed. She put on an old pair of shorts, a T-shirt and her old boots. Daddy and her Uncle Vince had already started rounding up the cows that would be going to the sale barn.

When the back screen door slammed and Daddy came in stomping grass off his barn boots, Aliza Rae excitedly tried to rush him up so they could go. But first was breakfast. Hot, fluffy biscuits, gravy, crisp bacon and eggs. The whole family sat, held hands and Daddy said the blessing. The smell of coffee was strong in Mama and Daddy's cups. The girls had tall, cold glasses of milk from the milking Daddy had done the night before. After breakfast, Laurel Jayne and Carley Anne helped Mama wash, dry and put away the dishes, but Aliza Rae got to skip today so she and Daddy could start the 50-mile trip to the sale barn. It felt like forever to get there and probably really did to Daddy since Aliza Rae chattered the whole way there. Once they arrived, Daddy checked in and the two cows in the trailer were released into the large pen where they were corralled into individual pens with other cows their size. Daddy and Aliza Rae walked up the narrow, wooden stairway to the walkway which made a middle square with walkways out each direction. They saw the cows, pigs and goats in pens underneath them. Aliza Rae tried to find their two cows and excitedly pointed them out to Daddy when she saw them. They saw big bulls, small calves, pigs and goats of all sizes and Aliza Rae picked out her favorites. After a while, they went into the center arena that was surrounded by rows of bleachers. They sat among the crowd of men, children and sometimes wives. Daddy warned Aliza Rae that once the bidding started, she would need to be still and quiet so she wouldn't accidentally buy a cow! The auctioneer started the bidding as the first cow was released into the arena. It ran in circles as a man with a prod would poke it to make it show its best side. After a bit, Aliza Rae would get tired and lay her head in Daddy's lap and nap best she could. Almost all the women had cardboard "church fans" and the breeze they created with the fans felt good. Finally, one of Daddy's cows would be brought out and the bidding would start as Daddy tapped Aliza Rae's shoulder to wake her up. After both cows had sold, they got up, stretched their legs and headed to the office to pick up a check. Next came Aliza Rae's favorite part. Hamburgers, fries and sweet tea in the sale barn restaurant. After lunch, they would head back home, Daddy humming to the gospel songs on the radio and Aliza Rae stretched out on the truck seat sound asleep.

Chapter 3

Jake and Sissy were busy raising three girls in a five-year span. When Laurel Jayne was born, one leg was slightly shorter than the other. Sissy had to put four cloth diapers on her at a time, so laundry day and hanging clothes on the line was time consuming but an act of love. When Laurel Jayne was three, her doctor decided it was time for surgery. The surgery was done in Greenville, SC and she wore a full leg cast for a few months while her leg healed. When she woke up from surgery, Jake and Sissy could hear her crying all the way down the hall because she thought they had cut her leg off. The nurse took her baby doll that Great Grandmother Ethel had left her, wrapped toilet paper around its leg, then removed it to show her the doll's leg was still there. Laurel Jayne went on to keep that doll even after she was grown. The months following the surgery were filled with at home therapy to make sure the leg healed properly. There were also annual visits to the doctors in Greenville until Laurel Jayne was in her teens. Carley Anne was born when Laurel Jayne was three, so it was a difficult but wonderful time.

Many days during that time felt like a never-ending cycle of laundry, cooking and caring for her little ones. When Carley Anne was six weeks old, the family made the trip to Toccoa for her checkup and then went to Carnesville to spend the night with Granny and Granddaddy Greene. They leaned a chair back to make Carley Anne a bed. She got choked from a stuffed-up nose and could not breathe despite her parents and grandparents' efforts to help her. She had to be rushed to the doctor down the road to have her nose suctioned out to enable her breathing to normalize. It was a scary moment for everyone, and Mama didn't sleep at all that night as she watched

Carley Anne breathe. She became especially aware of future problems and the suction syringe was a constant item in the diaper bag until Carley Anne was old enough to blow her nose. Sissy spent hours moving and stretching Laurel Jayne's legs and many hours rocking Carley Anne in the rocking chair pulled up near the heater and rubbing her feet with Lee's Save the Baby to ease the stuffy nose she always seemed to have. That always stuffy nose earned her the nickname Snuffy. Laurel Jayne's nickname was Grubby and, while no one seemed to remember who gave it to her or why, Uncle Vince called her that long into adulthood. Later on, Aliza Rae would earn the nickname Miss Magoo after a cartoon character who was always getting into some sort of mishap.

One night during this trying time, Sissy woke up to hear Laurel Jayne crying in her bed. She went in to see what was wrong and, in the dark, asked Laurel Jayne why she was crying. "My sides hurt, Mama!" said Laurel Jayne. Perplexed, Sissy turned on the light and learned that Laurel Jayne had mumps. This was the first of many normal childhood illnesses that Mama would nurse her babies through.

With Jake working to support his little family and Sissy's momma living 50 miles away, Sissy took on the task of keeping the home and raising her babies with sometimes only the support of her in-laws up the hill. Her family was supportive and helped as much as they could with the kids. On one visit, Aliza Rae refused to eat because she had to be held instead of being put in a highchair. Granddaddy Horace went right out and bought her a highchair. Even though he had 3 kids and 4 grandkids, he didn't want the baby to be disciplined if she wouldn't eat the next time they were there. He called and said, "you tell that baby that Granddaddy bought her a chair."

Jake was one of four children. Elbert was the oldest boy, and the girls were

Caroline and Charmaine. Caroline and
Elbert both lived nearby with their
families. When Laurel Jayne was born,
Caroline had Lynette and Elbert's wife had
Hannah, so the three cousins born in a
two-week span were instant friends.
Elbert's wife had a boy and a girl before
Hannah and three more girls after.
Caroline had another girl a few years after
Lynette. Charmaine, the youngest
daughter, had a baby girl that died at birth
and then a son.

Sissy was the only girl and had two
brothers, Charlie who was older and Alan
who was born when Sissy was 13. Charlie
was Sissy's protector and Sissy was
Alan's second momma, so by the time she
had babies of her own, she was
comfortable in the momma role. Charlie
went on to marry Betsy and they had three
children, Eric, Davy and Darcy. Alan
married Cathy and they had no children.

Sissy didn't learn to drive until Aliza
Rae was in fifth grade, so most days it
was just her and the babies. She

remembered fondly walks to the top of the hill when the girls would constantly be trying to outdo each other in commanding Mama's attention. This was not because they didn't already have Mama's attention. They just soaked up all of their parents' love and devotion to them like little sponges and thrived as a result.

One Fall day, Laurel Jayne was telling Mama all she had learned in Sunday School that week. "God made the flowers, didn't he Mama?" "Yes, Laurel Jayne, God made the flowers," said Mama. "God made the trees, didn't he Mama?" said Laurel Jayne. "Yes, Laurel Jayne, God made the trees," said Mama. This went on for a while with bugs, birds, sky and all of God's wonders. "God made the sunshine, didn't he Mama?" continued Laurel Jayne. Before Mama could answer, Carley Anne piped up and said, "And God made the moonshine too, didn't he Mama?" Mama stifled a giggle, so she didn't hurt Carley Anne's feelings. "Yes,

Carley Anne, God did indeed make the moonshine too."

Thus began years of fierce sisterhood. The girls were competitive with each other, but with everyone outside the family, they were and always would be each other's strongest supporter and always have each other's back.

Chapter 4

"Please, Mama, can't I just stay home with you and Carley Anne? I can help take care of her", Laurel Jayne pleaded as she, Mama and Carley Anne walked up the hill to meet the bus. Since neither the bus driver nor the mailman made the trip down the dirt road to the Hubbard home, daily treks to the top of the hill were the norm. That old dirt road was a central part of their lives.

Laurel Jayne did not like going to school, much preferring to be home with Mama and Carley Anne. Many days she would plead with Mrs. Palmer, her kind and patient teacher, to call Mama to come get her. She didn't understand that wasn't possible. It tore at Sissy's heartstrings to know that her baby girl was unhappy, but she knew it was necessary. There were many days when the bus driver would flag down Jake or Uncle Vince on their way home from their night shift jobs because Laurel Jayne was crying and was inconsolable.

Once Carley Anne started school it was better for a while. Laurel Jayne just naturally took on the role of second mama to her siblings, so she felt a sense of responsibility in making sure Carley Anne got to her class and onto the bus in the afternoon. That seemed to take her mind off her own unhappiness. That eased Sissy's worries since by this time she had another baby at home to care for and the days were full and passed quickly before it was once again time to meet the bus at the top of the hill, help with homework and get supper on the table. Unfortunately, Laurel Jayne's school happiness was short-lived, and she had another tough time the next year. By now, her unhappiness had worn off on Carley Anne, who would often play sick in an effort to stay home. Because of her history with congestion, it was difficult to tell if she was really in the early stages of another bout of sickness or if she was pretending to be sick. She would be "sick" until the bus ran and then was content to play quietly with her Barbies or watch tv and have Mama bring her lunch on a tray. Mama made the best ice chips to bring down fever! She would wrap the ice cubes in a washcloth and beat them with a meat cleaver until they were all crushed and then put them in a glass for the sick child to crunch on. There were also Kool-Aid popsicles made in the Tupperware popsicle set. They were the best on sweltering Georgia summer days.

Finally, Jake and Sissy decided something had to be done about Carley Anne's behavior. The next time she was "sick" she was made to stay in bed all day. No playing with toys, no tv, no attention from Mama except when she brought her lunch on a tray. The Hubbard girls did not enjoy laying around all day and from that day forward Carley Anne willingly went to school.

When the time came for Aliza Rae to go to school, Sissy felt a sense of dread about the familiar reaction of her girls. As the baby, she knew it might be even harder for Aliza Rae to be away from her all day. But when the first day of school arrived, Aliza Rae went happily with no tears and wanting no help from her sisters. Sissy would always say about Aliza Rae "she was the most independent of all my children from day one." Years later, Aliza Rae would say about Sissy, "she always said I was independent, but I know that was just a nice way of saying stubborn." While the school independence was a good thing, it probably was also an indicator of high-spirited, stubborn, often reckless behavior to come.

All the girls were good students and brought home good grades. Mrs. Palmer was also Aliza Rae's first grade teacher and was most likely surprised by the differences in her personality and Laurel Jayne's. Laurel Jayne and Carley Anne were obedient and polite. Aliza Rae was a rule tester. In high school, she often got into tiffs with her Home Economics teacher. Laurel Jayne was an excellent seamstress and Carley Anne could make perfect biscuits. Aliza Rae had to rip stitches out of her romper assignment so many times it was practically threadbare and many of her biscuits ended up burned and in the trash. Aliza Rae preferred Small Engine Repair and Horticulture classes to Home Economics, Shorthand and Typing. It seemed that all efforts to point her toward classes intended to make girls into well-rounded women were in vain when it came to the tomboy that was Aliza Rae Hubbard.

Chapter 5

Aliza Rae was having a bad week. Their
church was having Fall revival. Usually it
was an exciting time because, after
evening service, some of the families they
were friends with would come to their
house or they would go to theirs. This
usually happened on Friday night or
maybe even on a school night if the
service let out early enough. They would
eat big bowls of popcorn and the kids
would play games while the parents
talked. But this week started off on a bad
note when the Hubbards had preachers,
theirs and the visiting preacher, over for
supper on Monday night. It was
customary for the families to host the
preachers each day of revival for dinner
and supper. Mama fixed spaghetti, which
was one of Aliza Rae's favorites. They sat
down at the table, Daddy said the
blessing, the preachers were served and

FINALLY Mama piled spaghetti onto Aliza Rae's plate. She wrapped a few strands loosely on her fork, held the fork over her head and slurped the spaghetti slowly into her mouth. Going in for the second bite, she happened to look toward Mama, who gave her a disapproving look and a slight shake of her head. She couldn't imagine what that was about, so she got another forkful and started her "fork over the head, slurp the spaghetti into her mouth" routine again. This time she caught Daddy's disapproving look. Aliza Rae was perplexed. What was she doing wrong? Daddy's rule was you don't have to eat what is fixed, but you aren't getting anything else. None of the Hubbard girls were picky eaters as a result of that rule. Plus, Mama was an excellent cook. The only thing Aliza Rae could remember hating was when Mama fixed mashed turnips and Aliza Rae thought it was mashed potatoes, so she put a big serving of them on her plate and then had to finish them. Yuck! But she was definitely enjoying her spaghetti. The preachers had to get to the church and when they left, Daddy gave her a spanking! Turns out, slurping your spaghetti instead of using your manners to eat politely was another rule for the table. Aliza Rae was heartbroken. Usually all Daddy had to do was tell her he was disappointed in her and she straightened up. She hated disappointing Daddy. So actually getting a spanking from him just set the tone for the whole week.

On Tuesday, Aliza Rae decided to wear her white turtleneck bodysuit with her orange and brown striped pants and her brown cardigan sweater. It was one of her favorite outfits. She loved her first-grade teacher, Mrs. Palmer and she had a first-grade crush on a shaggy-haired boy named Kevin Cauthen. Kevin had golden skin, brown hair that was cut in a bowl cut and hung down almost to his eyes. He had already started losing his baby teeth and missing three of them just made him cuter to Aliza Rae. Not going to kindergarten and starting first grade at five years old, she was a little younger than the others in her class, so she still had all her baby teeth, so Kevin seemed "worldly" to her.

By midmorning, Aliza Rae noticed a pick on the belly of her body suit. She tried to pull it loose but that just made it worse. As the yarn started to unravel, Aliza Rae kept pulling, thinking it would eventually stop. She asked to go to the restroom where she kept pulling the thread. By the time Aliza Rae realized it was too late, she was wearing a long-sleeved turtleneck halter that was still snapped in her pants. Thankfully, she was wearing her cardigan, so she buttoned it up making sure the mound of thread was hidden underneath. When she got back to her desk, it was time for recess, so as everyone was scrambling for jackets, she quietly took out her safety scissors, snipped the yarn thread and hid the whole bundle in her book satchel. For the rest of the day, Aliza Rae had to wear her sweater buttoned up. When Mama met their bus at the top of the hill, Aliza Rae showed her the damage. At first Mama was a little exasperated. Aliza Rae was so rough on clothes. Thank goodness most everything she wore was a hand-me-down. But once Aliza Rae tearfully told Mama what happened, she couldn't help but laugh.

On Thursday, Aliza Rae's class went to lunch just like any other day. They had the spoon burgers and apple crisp Aliza Rae loved. Lunch at their elementary school wasn't fancy, only one choice of main dish plus one side but the cookies were amazing. When lunch was over, Mrs. Palmer stayed behind to get a refill of sweet tea. Aliza Rae thought that would be the grandest thing and reason enough to become a teacher, just for the tea. Aliza Rae wasn't line leader that day, so she got into line in the middle with the other H's. When they got back to the room, instead of going to their desk and sitting quickly, the kids were all running around the room and yelling while three kids stood on the counter and watched out the windows along the ceiling, warning the kids when Mrs. Palmer made the turn down the hallway. Aliza Rae wanted to impress Kevin with her bravery, so she volunteered. By the time Mrs. Palmer came back to the room, all the kids were sitting quietly at their desks. But they didn't know she could hear them from the end of the hall. She knew of their scheme to watch out for her, so she asked the class who the lookouts were. Tattling quickly ensued and Aliza Rae found herself in the hall for 30 minutes with two other classmates. When the principal, Mr. Collins walked by, she just knew she was done for, but he kept walking. Mrs. Palmer sent a note home which resulted in a spanking from Mama. Two in one week! For a family where spankings were rare, Aliza Rae was having quite the week. She managed to stay out of the hall until Mr. Cannon's seventh grade Science class where most everyone spent time in the hall at some point. Mr. Cannon had no time for nonsense as he would tell you.

By the time Friday rolled around, all the frustrations of the week were forgotten. Revival wrapped up and family friends came to the Hubbards for popcorn afterward. All was right in Aliza Rae's world again.

Chapter 6

Gertrude Greene was known to everyone as "Koot". She was Sissy's grandmother on her daddy's side and to the Hubbard girls and their cousins, she was Granny Koot. They didn't realize when they were younger that they were blessed not only to still have their great grandmother, but to have a great-grandmother who was still so active and loved it when her great grandkids visited. Aliza Rae, Carley Anne, Laurel Jayne and Charlie's daughter Darcy would spend a week at a time with her, exploring the big old white house with porches all around and running and playing in the surrounding yard and pasture. Granny Koot lived above Granny and Granddaddy Greene until they moved just down the road a little way. She lived until she was 90, passing away when Aliza Rae was a young adult. She was a strong, independent woman long before it was the norm. She was mischievous and had a wonderful sense of humor. When she was a young girl, her mailman was terrified of dogs, so she would hide in the bushes and do a wonderful barking impression, sending him running down the road with the mail flying in the air behind him.

As a young married woman, Gertrude was eager to start a family. However, after Horace Anderson Greene was born, she took one look at her husband and told him if there were any more babies, he would have to have them. Since that was impossible, Horace was an only child.

Horace grew up and met the love of his life, Frances Lauretta Elizabeth McMurray, when they were just teenagers. When they decided to marry, they were too young, so they drove to the next town and lied about their ages and started life together eventually raising Sissy, Charlie and Alan. As they were leaving town after their wedding, Horace somehow managed to entangle his car in the town's

Christmas tree lights and drag the lit tree behind them all around the town square. So much for staying lowkey about lying about their ages!

When the Hubbard girls came along, they loved going to stay with Granny Koot in the big old white farmhouse she and Granddaddy Grady lived in during their marriage. It was a magical place for a child, surrounded by numerous porches, all sorts of flowers thanks to Gertrude's green thumb, and numerous outbuildings where kids could play. There was a well where water could be drawn up in a bucket and drank from a metal dipper. It was the coldest, most refreshing drink on sweltering summer Georgia days. The girls and Charlie and Betsy's daughter Darcy would run and play and explore the old attic, which had many old books, hats and clothing and all sorts of other items used for imaginative play. For breakfasts, Granny Koot would make the girls canned biscuits slathered in butter and coffee that was half sugar and half coffee. When it was time for bed, Darcy, Laurel Jayne and Carley Anne would sleep in one of the beds and send Aliza Rae to sleep in the other one with Granny Koot. Those were sleepless nights for a little girl who thought her great grandmother was really old and would die in the bed with her.

For many years, a friend of Granddaddy Grady's named Elee lived with them. He was disabled and used a wheelchair which was stored in the attic after his death. Laurel Jayne, Carley Anne and Darcy convinced Aliza Rae that Elee's ghost could be heard bumping down the stairs at night. Aliza Rae would often lie awake next to Granny Koot, listening for the sound of her breathing and for the thumping of a wheelchair on the stairs. On hot summer nights, Granny Koot would sleep with her feet hanging out the window which created more anxiety for Aliza Rae, who worried that some sort of critter might make its way in.

But while the nights were a little scary, the days were magical. Granny

Koot did have one vice. At some point, she started smoking Kool cigarettes, but like most good Southern women, she hid her habit. She kept the cigarettes hidden in her dishtowel drawer and thought nobody knew why she would disappear a few times a day and smoke would boil from the cracks of the old outhouse. She was a smoker for years, but no one mentioned it to her, even when her great-granddaughters happened to see the smoke one day and frantically ran to tell their parents. Smoking was her only vice, and she was a wonderful, much-loved mother, grandmother and great-grandmother who created wonderful, lifelong memories for her girls.

In the "front room", the parlor, there was fancy furniture and a piano that Granny Koot would play for the girls. She had a plastic bunny bank and a stackable track that you could race marbles down. But probably the most fun was the rows of cubbies built into the wall where the girls could play post office and sort the pieces of paper they fashioned into mail. She would make Jiffy popcorn to snack on. The fact that her driver's license had lapsed was of no concern to Granny Koot on the occasions when she and the girls would pile into her old car and go for long car rides, looking at the various plants and flowers along the way.

One of Aliza Rae's favorite memories was when Granny Koot would come to Cleveland to stay while Mama, Laurel Jayne and Carley Anne would go to 4-H camp. Every afternoon, Aliza Rae would pick a story from the Childcraft books, and she and Granny Koot would settle onto the front porch swing with bowls of dry corn flakes topped with a spoonful of sugar and glasses of iced sweet tea and Granny Koot would read the story doing impressions of Billy Goat Gruff, The Big Bad Wolf or The Three Little Pigs.

Those days with Granny Koot were some of the best for Jake and Sissy's girls and years later they would realize what a true blessing it was to have her in their lives.

Chapter 7

Summers at that little house on the dirt road were the best. The cousins, Lynette, Cici and Dan stayed with Sissy and the girls while their mommas worked. The price of babysitting was cookies and Kool-Aid, both staples of childhood. Sissy would make a big pitcher of Kool-Aid each week and the kids would enjoy a paper cupful with a handful of butter cookies after a hot and tiring game of kickball, Red Rover or Kick the Can. Many a kickball was lost to the barbed wire fence in those days.

Summer days were spent outside. The adventures started the minute the cousins arrived IF they were lucky. Often mornings started in the garden, picking beans or squash from rows of plants that seemed to go on for miles. Jake and Sissy believed in giving back for what God had blessed them with and they gave away 5-gallon buckets of veggies or apples, berries and grapes. Other mornings started by pulling on boots and traipsing through knee-high grass trying to corral a cow or group of cows that made their escape through a hole in the barbed wire fence. There was always a moment of fear as a cow would inadvertently run toward the girls instead of toward the open gate. But finally it would make that turn, the gate would be cleared and later on Daddy and Uncle Vince would make the needed repairs to the spot in the fence where the cow or cows escaped. This was a process that repeated itself pretty regularly. Jake's cows were very tame due to the amount of time he spent with them. Aliza Rae loved to go to the barn with Jake when he milked the cow. At one time they had a cat that would hang out close by and Jake would squirt milk straight from the cow into the cat's mouth!

The girls made so many memories on those hot summer days with the cousins.

There were the usual squabbles that Sissy had to settle, but for the most part they whiled away the days playing games, playing in the playhouses they created, riding bikes and playing in the creek on really hot days. They would find big rocks and pile them up to make dams to make the creek water high enough to swim in, or at least high enough to lay in and stay cool.

One day, while all the adults were working in the hayfield, the cousins were all playing in the backyard at Vince and Charmaine's. Dan and Vince had put up a tent, hammering the metal stakes into the hooks on the tent to keep it in place. The cousins were playing house, but with a weird twist. They pretended that the housekeeper had met with a bad fate and died and came back to haunt them. As the "housekeeper" banged on the outside of the tent, Carley Anne bravely unzipped the door and went out. The housekeeper started chasing her around the tent. Carley Anne slipped on the grass and fell, slicing her knee open with one of the metal tent stobs. One of the cousins ran to get the adults and several of them piled into the car to take Carley Anne to Doc Edwards office for stitches. Later they talked about what a mess they must have been, all arriving sweaty and dirty from the hayfield and Carley Anne leaving a dirty ring around the pillow that Doc Edwards nurse gave her to hug while stitches were put in.

Riding bikes was a regular activity for the girls and for the cousins. They would ride as long as they could still pedal and then push their bikes the rest of the way up the long hill, then hop on, take their feet off the pedals as soon as they got up speed and then ride down as fast as they could feeling the wind in their hair. Having the bicycle chain pop off was a regular occurrence so if that happened they just had to hold on and hope they didn't meet a car before they got to the bottom of the hill. The girls would sometimes ride their bikes to the mailbox at the top of the hill in the early morning and put a piece of mail in that Sissy needed to go out. When they did, they would often wear their gowns and housecoats. On more than one occasion, the bottom of Aliza Rae's housecoat would end up caught in the bicycle chain and tear. Eventually, Sissy would put an end to that practice!

On the dirt road, there were two bridges that covered the creeks. They were made of wood boards with gaps between each board. When the girls stood on them, they could see the creek below. Aliza Rae would always walk her bike across because she thought the Billy Goat Gruff lived underneath the bridge and would grab her and eat her when her bicycle tire would get caught in the gaps.

One summer day between third and fourth grade, Aliza Rae went with her sisters on their bikes to the mailbox. Aliza Rae rode out to Granny and Pa's to get their mail for them. As Sissy would tell it later, Laurel Jayne came running into the house yelling "Mama, Aliza Rae is laying in the road and she's not moving!" Sissy looked out the window and took off running up the hill. As she reached Aliza Rae, she would later say, her baby girl sat up and started moaning in pain. She picked Aliza Rae up and carried her the rest of the way to Granny and Pa's where they rushed her to Doc Edwards' office. Thankfully, Granny Koot was visiting and stayed with the older girls. It turned out that as Aliza Rae was coming back down the hill on her bike, a rock flew out from under the tire and hit Aliza Rae square in the middle of her forehead, knocking her out cold and causing her to fall off her bike and land face first on the dirt road. Her teeth were buried into her gums, which was a blessing because she didn't lose any teeth as a result of the wreck. Doctor Edwards told Sissy the damage to Aliza Rae's face was worse than most motorcycle wrecks he had seen and that evening when Jake got home from work, Sissy went out on the porch to prepare him before he came in and saw his little girl. Thankfully, Aliza Rae only had one stitch right under her nose and minor scarring that would stay with her for life as a reminder of that day. Aliza Rae didn't remember anything about the accident and only remembered that when she woke up on the couch later that afternoon, her sisters and Granny Koot and Mama had made her a big poster board get well card and she got a doll that she had been admiring for weeks at the dime store. The downside was that, because of the injuries to her mouth, for several days she could not eat solid food and had to live on a diet of Carnation Instant Breakfast. Sissy would fix a glass and set it on the table next to the couch and as soon as she went outside or to the back room to do something, Aliza Rae would pour the majority of it down the sink. Aliza Rae would never drink Carnation Instant Breakfast again after that time.

Not long after, Sissy learned to drive so she never had to rely on others in an emergency again. Carrying an eight-year-old up a big hill was a great lesson.

When they weren't riding bikes, the girls and the cousins were usually in their playhouses dreaming big imaginative story lines. There was one playhouse in the old pig pen that hadn't housed pigs in many years. There was usually a New York apartment in the girls bedroom and the main playhouse on one side of the dirt floor smokehouse. Jake and Sissy let the girls paint pictures on the inside walls and the girls kept their plastic tea sets there and fixed elaborate meals consisting of Mimosa tree "beans", dog fennel weed mashed potatoes and french fries and mud pies.

The kids would often play in the different playhouses in groups of two. One day, Aliza Rae and Dan left their house in the old pig pen and took the baby to visit Carley Ann and Cici in their high-rise apartment in the girls bedroom. While they visited, Carley Anne put the baby in the next room to sleep. When the time came to leave, Carley Anne brought the baby back and said "something is terribly wrong! The baby must be very sick!" "What do you mean?" asked Aliza Rae. Carley Anne pulled back the baby's blanket. "Look! She has a horrible rash!" Carley Anne had taken a red marker and drawn dots all over the baby's face. "I'm telling Mama!" yelled Aliza Rae. She and Dan took the baby and left, so angry that Carley Anne had ruined her favorite doll. Aliza Rae refused to play with Carley Anne for several days, but it would be several months before Aliza Rae was able to get even with Carley Anne by burning her favorite baby doll's hair off by sticking its head in the gas heater.

The girls shared the majority of their toys, which consisted of a few baby dolls, tea sets and a big citrus fruit box that housed their Barbie, PJ, Midge, Alan and Ken dolls, a few pieces of furniture and many tiny outfits Sissy had painstakingly sewed. There was also a Barbie Dreamhouse. Rainy afternoons the girls would take the Barbie box onto the back porch and set up homes on the freezer where they would play for hours.

The girls were usually careful with their toys because there was not a lot of extra money to spend on toys. There were a few times when carelessness led to tragedy like the time the baby doll Thumbelina was accidentally left outside, and the pig ate her nose. Or the time Aliza Rae cut Midge's hair thinking it would grow back. The only toy that Aliza Rae was especially careful with though was a blue and white stuffed rabbit she named Binky after her Uncle Alan's childhood imaginary friend. Though he would eventually lose most of his stuffing and his ears went limp, Aliza Rae carried Binky with her into adulthood.

Aliza Rae had no problem with playing by herself if her sisters or cousins were not around. Daddy gave her an old 4x4 wood beam, which she would prop up off the ground-one end on the porch step and one end on a chair. There she would create and perform balance beam routines and pretend she was a gymnast. On rainy days, she would take the old tin kitchen water cup out to the porch and play church, using the cup to take up a collection by catching the rain drips off the porch roof. The more rain she collected, the better the "collection".

The girls definitely had vivid imaginations which they used to carry them through those blissful childhood days.

Chapter 8

Over the years, there were many pets on the family farm-some dogs, cats, horses and cows, some critters and bugs.

There was a big, fat bullfrog that would return to the playhouse every year. He became a family pet, and the girls named him Kermit. There would also be June bugs with strings tied to their legs to make a leash and lightning bugs caught on hot summer nights and put into jars with holes punched in the lids. Then they were placed on dressers in the girls bedroom, flickering and lighting up the room for a couple days until they were released back into the night sky. There were tadpoles caught from the pond and put into pie pans with water and mud in them. They would swim around until the day they turned into frogs and hopped out of the pan, never to be seen again. Other frogs were found in the yard and the girls would put them in boxes with powderpuff beds. Sissy never knew what she might find when she walked into the girls bedroom.

When Laurel Jayne was little, there was a dog named George who was very protective of her. "Get in the car, George", Laurel Jayne would say, and they would climb under the kitchen sink and close the door and play. One day Laurel Jayne disappeared. Sissy looked everywhere she could think of in the house to no avail. Suddenly she remembered the creek and she took off running. There sitting on the bank was Laurel Jayne and George. Sissy had never been so relieved and so mad at the same time.

When Aliza Rae was five, the family got a cat named Calico who lived until Aliza Rae's freshman year of college. Aliza Rae quickly claimed her as her own, giving her the nickname Callie. Callie was a tough girl, quickly adjusting to farm life. Once when she had tiny kittens to protect, the neighbor dog came around threatening the babies' lives. Callie fought him and the Hubbard's family dog, splitting their faces with her claws and sending them both running, yelping in pain.

When the girls were a little older, Laurel Jayne started asking for a pet gerbil. Against Sissy's better judgment, she finally gave in although she did not like anything rodent-like. They bought two gerbils and Laurel Jayne named them Laverne and Shirley after two of her favorite TV characters and she took great care of them as she had promised.

One day Shirley disappeared, and the girls searched the whole house for her. That evening as Sissy started to make biscuits for supper, she took the lid off the five-gallon container full of flour she kept inside a bottom cabinet and up popped Shirley completely covered in flour. She must have jumped in unseen early that morning during the breakfast biscuit prep.

One day as Laurel Jayne was cleaning the gerbil cage, she let them run around on the bed as she cleaned and added fresh shredded newspaper. The bedroom had a window that opened onto the back porch and Laurel Jayne smiled when she saw the cat sitting on the back porch freezer watching the gerbils from a safe distance. Unbeknownst to her, Mama had opened the back door to take something onto the porch and, fast as a lightning strike, the cat took off, ran through the house, grabbed up Laverne and ran back onto the porch with the gerbil's head hanging out one side of her mouth and her tail hanging out the other side. All the girls were screaming as Sissy grabbed the cat and pried the gerbil from her mouth. Laverne started running around the porch and finally ran behind the freezer. The cat was put outside, Sissy and the girls were finally able to corner Laverne and put her safely back in her home. The chaos finally subsided, and Sissy and the girls sat down and enjoyed a much-deserved glass of sweet tea.

One day Jake came home with a baby squirrel he had found all by itself. Aliza Rae promptly named her Shirley Squirrely and carried her around everywhere like a pet. She would climb up Jake's arm and nestle into his shirt pocket to sleep.

Over the years, the girls made great memories caring for their many pets, but they were also mindful of the fact that they lived on a farm and sometimes farm life wasn't pleasant.

A painful reminder of this occurred one day as Aliza Rae and Dan were walking up the dirt road from the Hubbard's to Granny and Pa's. As they walked, they passed Billy, the old goat who lived in the pasture. He frequently escaped like he had done on this particular day, but he never went far. He stood chewing on the grass on the bank, but suddenly started charging toward Aliza Rae and Dan with his head down and his horns up. "Run!" shouted Aliza Rae and both kids took off, but Billy was faster. As he caught up to them, Dan grabbed him by the horns and held him at arm's distance. Panicked, Aliza Rae said "OK, I'll count to three and we will run. Ready? 1....2....3...." but Dan couldn't let go or Billy would have caught him with his horns. Soon the kids screaming caught the attention of Uncle Vince, who was at the Hubbards trying to fix the tractor in the yard. The tractor was used for baling hay and bush hogging pasture weeds and numerous other tasks on the farm and making repairs was a frequent job. While Uncle Vince was working, he heard the screams of the kids and jumped in his truck. When he got to them, the only way to stop Billy was to stab him with his pocketknife. Billy took off and jumped back into the pasture. Sadly, the dogs found him there later, wounded and defenseless and killed him. The kids were beside themselves. No matter that he had senselessly tried to attack them, he was their pet before that day, and it was sad to know he died in that way.

In spite of the realities of farm life, their childhood furry friends would give the girls a love for animals that they would carry into adulthood.

Chapter 9

Days spent with the cousins at Pa and Granny's were special days indeed. Granny Hubbard had an impressive collection of salt and pepper shakers and Aliza Rae loved to sit at the kitchen table lining the shakers up and playing with them while munching on saltines topped with peanut butter and marshmallows and toasted to a perfect golden brown. There were all sorts of places for Aliza Rae and Dan to explore, including the old chicken house Pa used for storing every possible kind of tool and any item he happened to collect besides. It had a comforting smell of diesel fuel and tobacco and on rainy days it was a cozy place to play. There was the old barn where they would climb on the bales of hay and sit high above the ground and daydream. There was the tornado shelter built into the dirt bank, making it the coolest place to hang out on hot summer days. On lazy Sunday afternoons after church, the family would while away the hours on Granny and Pa's porch eating salted slices of watermelon or taking turns with the manual turn handle on the ice cream freezer until the peach or strawberry ice cream was a perfect consistency. There were ten concrete steps up to the porch and on the bottom porch Pa had etched the date and laid marbles spelling out the family name. There were mimosa trees for climbing until Dan fell out of one and broke his arm. There were games of horseshoes in the front yard for the men and pick up baseball games in the pasture for the kids, using boards for bases and another board with a handle cut into it for a bat. It wasn't uncommon for someone to accidentally slide into a cow manure pile while running the bases, which put the runner at an advantage because no one wanted to get close enough to tag them out!

But probably Aliza Rae's favorite place was the treehouse that Vince and

Jake built into the big oak tree in the pasture. Many years later, Aliza Rae would stand in that very spot with her parents, husband and kids and plan for the house they would build there. But first, there were long summer days of childhood where she and Dan would climb up, sprawl out on the floor of the treehouse and dream. "I'm going to live here forever", Aliza Rae would say. "I would rather live in a cave all my life than to live in the city." Little did she know how prophetic her words were and that one day she, her husband and her kids would move back to the only place she ever considered home.

Chapter 10

"Hurry girls, you are going to be late!" prodded Sissy. Aliza Rae was in second grade now and today was picture day at school and Sissy needed time to fix her hair. The girls rushed to make up their bed, putting their pajamas into the cute pajama bags that Mama had made for each of them. They zipped them up, tucked in the bed pillows, lined the pajama bags up at the top of the bed, and ran into the kitchen. Mama had fixed biscuits and gravy, bacon and eggs and tall glasses of milk. Breakfast was blessed and eaten quickly, teeth brushed, Laurel Jayne and Carley Anne pulled headbands into their just brushed hair while Mama put Aliza Rae's hair into dog ears and tied in ribbons that matched her peach Easter dress that had been carefully selected for picture day. Mama reminded Aliza Rae not to get too hot and dirty at recess since pictures inevitably were taken after recess. All three girls ran for the top of the hill to meet the bus and Sissy settled into her day's tasks which would quickly consume the day before meeting the bus at the top of the hill in the afternoon. There was comfort in the familiarity, the day-to-day routine. Sissy thrived in her role as momma and wife.

The girls came home that afternoon hungry and hot as usual after the bus ride. "Aliza Rae, what happened to your hair bow?" Sissy asked. Somehow, her youngest daughter had managed to lose one of the bows and no one bothered to take out the other one, making for a funny scene with the lopsided bow. "I don't know, I guess I lost it sometime today", said Aliza Rae and went about the business of changing into play clothes, eating her snack and doing her homework.

A few weeks later when the picture packages came back, there was Aliza Rae, one bow in and one missing. Sissy was so frustrated when she saw it, but for years to come it made for an interesting story and the picture was proudly put on display with Carley Anne and Laurel Jayne's.

There was never a dull moment with three energetic, imaginative girls to take care of. One day the girls decided they were hungry, and Mama was busy with some household task, so they took the big, glass jar of peanut butter and three spoons and went to the front porch to swing. As the three of them sat swinging as high as they could, one girl reached for the jar from another who wasn't quite ready to relinquish the jar and a squabble ensued. Suddenly, the jar crashed to the concrete floor and shattered glass and peanut butter became one big mess mixed together. Since all three were involved, all three got in trouble.

Another time, Daddy brought in a bucket of milk after milking the cow for the evening. The milk was poured into a glass gallon jug and put in the refrigerator. The next morning, Carley Anne got the gallon jug out, set it on the table and used a large metal spoon to go around the top of the jar to remove the thick layer of cream. This was a job usually reserved for Mama. She would pour off the cream, add sugar and vanilla and whip it until it formed peaks on the top. The whipped cream would then be added to peaches for dessert. In the winter if there was a rare Georgia snow, the cream would be used to make thick, delicious snow ice cream. But this particular morning, Carley Anne knew she could handle it. She wanted to show Mama she was a big helper. As she ran the spoon around the rim of the jug, the metal spoon slipped out of her hand and hit the bottom of the jug, cracking it open and sending the entire gallon of milk all over the table and kitchen floor. Not only was the milk wasted, but Mama also now had a huge mess to clean up. But she did so patiently as always, knowing that

Carley Anne had learned a big life lesson that morning.

Laurel Jayne quickly learned how to use her power as the oldest child to her advantage. When the girls were playing outside, Laurel Jayne would talk Carley Anne into touching the electric fence to see if it was on before they crossed into the pasture. One day Carley Anne had a cookie cutter from the playhouse in her hand and when she touched the fence with it, she got a jolt of electricity that taught her to never again touch an electric fence with a metal cookie cutter. When Laurel Jayne and Carley Anne wanted to change tv channels from one of the 3 stations their tv picked up to Channel 8, their favorite channel, they would tell Aliza Rae to "turn it to the channel with one fried egg on top of the other." One afternoon on the bus ride home, Laurel Jayne was eating a peanut butter sandwich left over from her lunchbox. She started picking on Aliza Rae and she stuck out her tongue with a chewed up peanut butter sandwich in her mouth. Aliza Rae had a weak stomach and started gagging and told Laurel Jayne she was telling Mama. Laurel Jayne begged her not to tell and told her she would give her the apple from her lunchbox if she didn't tell. But Laurel Jayne was also Carley Anne and Aliza Rae's biggest cheerleader and protector. It was one thing to pick on your own sisters, but when other people did it, that was cause enough to stick up for them. Sissy knew how to stop the girls' arguments pretty quickly with creative punishments like making them hug each other and say I love you to each other or separating them and putting one in each of three rooms in the house. Arguments never lasted long, and the girls would be best of friends again in no time. When the days were stressful, the family would take an evening walk hand-in-hand down the dirt road under the bright moon and in the cool evening air. Togetherness would bring calm and peace and they would then walk back home and get ready for bed. In the summer the girls would wear long t-shirts and, in the winter, flannel gowns. Once they had retrieved their pajamas from their pajama bags and put them on, they would pile on Mama and Daddy's king-sized bed and Daddy would read the Bible and pray. They girls would then say their bedtime prayers in their room and go to bed to sleep, nestled in their parents' love and dreaming happy dreams.

Chapter 11

Making the trip to Granny and Granddaddy Greene's always felt like a big adventure. It was 50 miles to Carnesville where they lived, which felt like a world away to the girls. Aliza Rae's weak stomach made car sickness very real for her and often she would have to be sick in the potty chair plastic bowl that Mama kept under the car seat for just such incidents.

Their grandparents took the Anderson Independent newspaper and Granny Greene always had a half-completed crossword puzzle from the paper on the kitchen table in the mobile home they lived in. She always made the most delicious homemade biscuits and butter beans. Granddaddy Horace would listen to his favorite gospel group on eight track tapes, bringing attention to his favorite upcoming song. The girls would make a playhouse of sorts in the little bedroom off the living room where they would play while they adults talked in the kitchen. Uncle Alan would always shower the girls with attention, taking them to the store and spending a quarter on each of them, letting them buy 25 pieces of penny candy even though his friends would tell him he was wasting his money. When Aliza Rae was in the 4th grade, her teacher decided that all girls needed to know how to put together a model car and all boys needed to know how to sew. Uncle Alan stayed up a whole night putting together the model car from the kit Sissy bought for Aliza Rae.

Uncle Alan loved his girls, and they loved him. They were in his wedding when he got married. Shortly after he was married, Mama got a phone call on the night of Aliza Rae's tenth birthday saying Alan and his best friend had been in a car wreck. Sissy and Jake hurriedly took the girls to stay with Vince and Charmaine and they made the fifty-mile trip to

Carnesville. Later that night, Dan and Aliza Rae were turning flips on the sleeping bags that Aunt Charmaine had laid out on the floor for the girls to sleep on. The phone rang and Aunt Charmaine went to the kitchen to answer it. The girls could hear her softly crying as she came back in the room to tell them that Uncle Alan had passed away. It was a sad time and one of the first family deaths the girls had experienced. Because he had been born when Sissy was thirteen and she had been a second momma to him, it was a difficult and sad time for the whole family. That first Christmas after his death earlier in the month, the family seemed to really recognize the importance of family and spending time together. Granddaddy Horace sat down on the floor to play with Aliza Rae with the toys she had gotten for Christmas. They made the best of a sad Christmas and held each other a little closer.

That was the first of several losses the Hubbard family would experience during the holiday season. Later on, all four grandparents would individually pass away during the holidays. This, more than most anything, made all of them know the importance of family and keeping them close and loving them with your entire being.

Chapter 12

Daddy had a way of making chores seem fun. The girls were always eager to help when it came time to harvest honey from the bees Daddy kept, although their "job" didn't start until Daddy brought the frames full of honeycomb into the house. Up until that point, they would watch from a safe distance as Daddy put on the beekeeper's outfit and used the smoker to calm the bees. Then they would wash and dry their hands really good and join Daddy as he set up the strainer and big pressure cooker on the back porch freezer, taking turns squishing the honey with their hands into the strainer as Daddy chopped in big squares of the honeycomb. The honey would drip into the pressure cooker and from there he would pour it into the jars he used for collection. Sometimes if a frame of honeycomb was particularly pretty, like the sourwood honey usually was, he would cut squares and put those directly into the jar before adding the honey from the bowl. There was nothing like that yummy sweet golden honey on Mama's homemade hot biscuits with butter.

In the summer, the girls would help in the garden picking beans, tomatoes, okra and squash. Daddy always picked the corn because it was difficult to know when it was ready just by looking at it. On more than one occasion, a new crop of watermelon plants would be dug up while weeding because the girls hadn't quite figured out how to differentiate between plants and weeds. But Daddy was always patient as he explained how to tell the difference. Picking tomatoes was fun, squash and okra was itchy, beans were just downright exhausting and exasperating. But when it came time to pick up potatoes, the girls were always ready. Daddy would hook the plow up to Chief, the big Appaloosa, and they would walk the potato rows digging up the plants and unearthing potatoes as they went. The girls pretended they were picking up Easter eggs and would see who could collect the most as the big five-gallon buckets they carried to put them into swung hitting their legs.

Daddy knew the names of all the plants and trees that grew on their property and the mountain behind it. Aliza Rae loved to walk with him up the mountain and have him call the names of trees and what purpose they served in woodworking, the plants and their medicinal purpose and the animals and insects and their purpose in the chain of life. Sometimes that would backfire though, such as the time that Laurel Jayne found and chewed rabbit tobacco right after a trip to the dentist for a teeth cleaning. Or the time Aliza Rae and Dan found wild onions growing in the yard while visiting family and ate to their heart's content, but then no one could stand to be within several feet of them for a couple days. But because they listened and learned which plants were safe and which were not, they didn't hesitate to partake of whatever they wanted in the yard. There was a type of clover that grew little pods that the girls called okra because it resembled the okra Daddy grew in the garden. The pods were sour and made for a nice treat.

There were family trips down the river in the metal boat with Daddy paddling and then they would stop, tie up to a tree and fish for a while, which meant yummy fried fish and homemade hushpuppies and fish gravy for supper. Those were fun times for Aliza Rae except for the time that Daddy told her to tie them up to a small tree at the river's edge and there was a snake in the tree! Aliza Rae, for all her love for critters, did not like snakes. Daddy laughed because he knew it was a harmless water snake, but Aliza Rae refused to tie up the boat after that.

Both Sissy and Jake were good stewards of what they had been given, were able to repurpose and reuse and not waste anything God had provided. They both worked hard to provide for their family in so many ways. While Daddy managed the farm, garden and yard, Mama managed their home. The girls had chores but mostly Mama ran her household single handedly. She was known for moving furniture frequently. Daddy would come home from work during the early morning hours and never knew where his bed might be. One day, while Mama was deep cleaning, she decided to flip the mattresses on the bed. All was well until she tried to flip the king-sized mattress on hers and Daddy's bed. She managed to get it turned up but got trapped under it on the way back down. Because the girls were outside playing and Daddy was on the couch sleeping, she lay under the mattress laughing for a while before she wriggled her way out. During the day, she would try to keep the girls quiet or send them outside to play while Daddy slept on the couch. The girls loved to play hairdresser and brush Daddy's hair and put in hair bows. The girls soaked up the knowledge their parents imparted. One day Daddy wanted a cup of hot tea and Carley Anne jumped at the chance to make it for him. Relying on her knowledge of watching Mama make a gallon of iced sweet tea, she put eight teabags in the cup and poured hot water over. Daddy took one sip and tried not to make a face and then proceeded to drink the entire cup while Carley Anne stood happily by.

Mama would sit at her sewing machine late in the evening after a full day's work around the house and finally getting the girls to bed. There she created masterpieces, from tiny Barbie clothes to baby doll clothes to matching Easter dresses and Christmas dresses for the girls and eventually even prom dresses. Once she made the girls matching shorts and cute bell sleeve tops that they wore on a rare family trip to Six Flags.

The family, especially Jake and Sissy, worked hard. But there were always fun times and special treats. Every Saturday night, Aliza Rae would hurry to get her bath and get her pajamas on. After supper dishes were done, she would settle down in front of the TV and watch The Muppets, laughing at the capers of the puppets. Then the entire family would watch Hee Haw and laugh at the jokes and sing along with the music. Sunday mornings the girls would hurry to get ready for church and then watch Davey and Goliath, Hercules and Gumby and Pokey. There was not a lot of TV watched in the Hubbard house as they all preferred to be outside or working on projects or playing. Besides, there were only three, sometimes four channels to watch if you could get the outside antenna rotated just right to pick up Channel 17.

Sometimes after church the family would treat themselves to burgers and fries at "Fat Pat's", a tiny restaurant in town. But most of the time the family ate delicious dinners that Sissy had cooked before church or on Saturday evening and then heated up for Sunday lunch. Sundays were a day of rest or visiting with family and friends nearby after church. Sometimes that meant visiting shut ins and delivering the tape-recorded sermon for the disabled or elderly person to listen to for a few days and sometimes it meant those lazy Sunday afternoons on Pa and Granny's porch and most always it meant a nap in the quiet bedrooms or on the couch. On chilly days, Aliza Rae loved to climb into the back seat of the car and nap in the warm sunshine.

There was not a lot of extra money for expensive vacations, but the girls never missed them. They did enjoy the Six Flags trip and a couple of trips to the beach, but they were just as happy or maybe even more so when the family made the trip to North Carolina to stay in the work in progress cabin that Granny Greene and Granddaddy Horace had bought. They also loved when Daddy would decide they should just take a drive into the mountain. They would pack the big green and tan picnic basket with sandwiches and containers of sweet tea and find a roadside picnic table to enjoy their lunch at on their adventure. On one of those trips, Daddy told the girls to watch as a dog in a yard was obviously about to chase their car. Daddy accelerated and the dog took off running across the yard. As soon as the dog passed their car, Daddy slowed down. The dog kept running for a second before looking back to see where the car was. He slowed down and Daddy sped up. The dog ran fast to catch up and as he passed the car, Daddy slowed down again. This went on for a minute or two and the whole family had a good laugh. Daddy had a wonderful sense of humor and loved a good laugh.

The girls grew to realize how much their parents sacrificed to create wonderful childhood memories for them, and their favorite thing was just spending time with their parents and each other.

No matter what was going on in or around the Hubbard home, there was always love and laughter involved.

Chapter 13

Shoal Creek Baptist Church was a central part of the Hubbard family's lives and the lives of the entire community. There was always something going on, whether it was regular Sunday morning services, Sunday evening services, Wednesday bible study, revival or Vacation Bible School.

Revival was held each season for one week and there were morning and night services with visiting preachers and singing groups, followed by those family get together popcorn or ice cream sessions.

Vacation Bible School was the highly anticipated event of the year for the girls, starting with the march-in, line up with appropriate classes, the pledge to the American flag, the Christian flag and the Bible. It was always a big treat to be asked to carry in the flag or Bible. Then there was the lesson of the night and crafts and snacks. There has never been a better snack than Bible School butter cookies with holes in the middle that a young girl could slip on her finger and pretend to be wearing a beautiful blingy ring. Add a paper cup of red cherry Kool-Aid and it was pretty much perfect. On Friday night, the last night of Bible School, commencement was held. All the parents would gather in the sanctuary and the kids would put on programs or recite Bible verses and sing songs they learned that week. Then they would all go to their classrooms where their macaroni necklaces, seashell art or construction paper masterpieces would be waiting in their chairs with their certificate of attendance. That was followed by little paper cups of ice cream with wooden spoons that left the ice cream tasting like the spoon but was still the highlight of the week.

Sunday mornings meant Sunday School class with Bible drills, when the teacher would call out a book, chapter and verse and the kids would race to see who could find it, stand and read it first. Aliza Rae was really good at Bible drills and once even was given a Bible as a gift for her efforts. She also had an attendance pin with little bridges with the particular year on them. The Hubbard Family rarely missed church, so the attendance pin was impressive. Aliza Rae wore it every Sunday morning. One Sunday morning, Aliza Rae accidentally stuck the hot end of a curling iron onto her eye, burning her eyeball and necessitating an emergency room visit. But because they made it back in time for preaching, the family still went to church only missing Sunday School. As stated, the Hubbard Family rarely if ever missed church.

The girls sang in the children's and youth choirs and once a week after school they would practice at the church. All the Shoal Creek kids that were in choir would ride the school bus to the church and practice.

The girls and their friends from church were always sleeping over at each other's houses. Usually after church, the girls and their friends would run back and forth between their parents talking in the church parking lot, begging their parents to let their friend come over or for them to go to another friend's house. Then they would stay up late laughing and talking and eating snacks. One particular sleepover at a friend's house, the girls took their sleeping bags out to the storage building, and they told ghost stories and laughed until the wee hours with all their friends. When they heard a noise outside, they were convinced there was a ghost, but it turned out the friend's dog had puppies under the storage building!

All of the Shoal Creek kids were really close and even after they were grown and gone, most all of them would make their way back for Homecoming each year, celebrating the church and the lifelong friendships they had made.

Chapter 14

Spending time with the cousins didn't just happen on those hot summer days. Once the girls were a little older and Mama went to work, Aliza Rae spent her summer days with Aunt Charmaine who, by this time, was unable to work at a normal job because of her arthritis. Both Aunt Charmaine and Aunt Caroline suffered from the crippling disease, but both were upbeat and optimistic and rarely if ever complained.

Aliza Rae and Dan would often beg Aunt Charmaine to take them to the swimming pool at the local motel in town. She would bargain with them and say once they had finished helping clean the house or whatever chore might need done but was difficult for her, she would take them to the pool. Many hours were spent splashing around and whiling away the hours there. On the days that Aliza Rae would spend the night, there would be

Little Debbie cookies and frozen Mello Yellos to enjoy before bedtime. Aliza Rae loved this treat, since Mama never bought soft drinks.

Some days the girls would spend the night with Lynette and Cici. Caroline's husband, Uncle Bill, was a quiet man. He smoked a pipe, and the house would have a distinctive, wonderful smell of clean house and pipe smoke. When the girls would wake up in the mornings, Aunt Caroline would have biscuits and chocolate gravy ready for them. What an extravagant treat! Aliza Rae thought there was nothing better than chocolate gravy.

On Halloween, the cousins, aunts and uncles would pile into the old wagon and Uncle Vince or Daddy would pull them with the tractor and they would go around the community trick-or-treating. Because the houses were so spread out, going to neighboring houses took some time but the kids would come back home happy and full of candy. There were camping trips and holidays and everyday life done together. The family was close and enjoyed each other's company.   Cousins are a special gift to be enjoyed. They never lost sight of the blessing of family.

Chapter 15

Christmas brought a plethora of warm memories for the Hubbards. The season started with the Christmas program at church with a nativity scene and singing and Santa would always make a visit and bring little gifts. Next on the list would be Christmas caroling in the wagon with family and friends. Everyone would pile into the wagon and sit on bales of hay, and someone would drive the tractor and pull the wagon around the community caroling, followed by hot chocolate with lots of marshmallows. On Christmas Eve night, they would pile into the car and drive around looking at Christmas lights and then come home to cookies and milk. They did not have a fireplace until later years, so every year the girls would take knee high socks and Mama would turn the three-legged piano stool upside down and the "stockings" would be hung. On Christmas morning, they would dump out the oranges, nuts, small toys and a single canned Coke, which was a huge treat for the girls.

The girls would find their pile of clothing and toys and spend the morning trying things on and playing with their toys. Mama would make stacks of warm, fluffy blueberry pancakes for breakfast and after they ate, the family would spend a quiet, lazy day celebrating and enjoying the day. Sometimes they would go to their grandparents in the afternoon.

Aliza Rae got many wonderful toys over the years, but her favorites were probably dolls and doll trunks, a Fisher Price village when she was 10, a little desk with three sides-one for pegs, one for chalk and one for magnets. It came with the pegs, chalk and a whole alphabet and numbers 0-9 magnets to stick on the board. But probably her favorite gift of all was the year she begged for a trampoline and got a pogo stick. Her parents and Santa knew best. Aliza Rae spent hours each summer trying to break her own record for number of jumps and would actually scrape bruises on the inside of her legs from the screw that held the pogo stick in place.

Carley Anne's favorite Christmas gift was a metal dollhouse with tiny furniture and a little plastic family.

But even more than the toys and clothes, the memories made with their family meant everything to the Hubbard family.

Chapter 16

As the girls grew and needed more space, Sissy and Jake built a bedroom and game room onto their house, finally having that fireplace they didn't have when the girls were younger. The girls helped Daddy mix the concrete and lay the brick for the fireplace, which was a lot of work but brought a sense of accomplishment.

That year, Aliza Rae and Carley Anne had a combined birthday party/sleepover with more friends than they had ever had overnight at the same time. There was plenty of room in the game room for all their sleeping bags lined up. Mama made them a birthday cake shaped like a train with peppermint candy wheels. It was so big it had to be positioned on two pieces of cardboard covered with aluminum foil. The girls spent the night laughing and talking about boys and eating. Daddy had gone hunting, probably to escape all the silliness. But by the time he returned to the house, the girls had moved on to telling ghost stories. Suddenly they heard the front door open. They were in the game room with the door shut, so they sat frozen and trying to be quiet. Suddenly the game room door opened, and a hand reached around and turned on the light. The girls all screamed, and Sissy came running and they all laughed as they realized it was just Jake coming home from hunting.

Sissy and Jake moved into the new bedroom and, as the oldest, Laurel Jayne moved from the double bed bedroom the girls were outgrowing into Sissy and Jake's old bedroom. Carley Anne and Aliza Rae continued to share a bedroom until Laurel Jayne went away to college and then Carley Anne moved into Laurel Jayne's bedroom. Eventually Aliza Rae moved into that bedroom when Carley Anne went to college and the extra bedroom was used for weekends home from college or for guests. Life was moving on past and, as teenagers and young adults, the girls went through the same stages as other teens and young adults. There were times when Aliza Rae's sharp words or indifference or defiant behavior likely broke her parents' hearts, but they just continued to pray daily for all three of their girls and the families they would one day have. God continued to be the center of every thought and every decision. Eventually, as the girls all started lives of their own, they realized anew what they never really forgot. All that really matters is family and love. They never really strayed far from home, either in the physical or the emotional. They knew that the old saying is true. Love grows best in small houses. And that little bit of heaven at the bottom of that old dirt road on Rural Route Two? Well, it's still standing and still growing love.

"Love grows best in little houses,
With fewer walls to separate.
Where you eat and sleep so close
Together, you can't help but communicate.
If we had more room between us, think of
All we'd miss.
Love grows best in little houses just like this."

Thank you for taking the time to read 'A Little Bit of Heaven on Rural Route Two'. It was written to honor the memories of my childhood. My parents and my sisters all provided memories to be included and I did my best to ensure that I relayed them accurately. I may have embellished a bit in spots or miscommunicated, considering I was not born yet for many of their memories.

I am so blessed to have such a loving, lifelong relationship with my family, and I never take that for granted. If I could offer any advice to someone reading this who might not be in a good place with their family, it would be to mend those relationships before it's too late. Especially in the case of siblings, there is no relationship that will be more longstanding. They are there from the time the last one of you is born until the first one of you dies. In most cases, you will be family longer than you and your parents, you and your spouse, you and your children. Don't let anything hinder that if you can help it.

I wish you, my wonderful reader, all of life's blessings.

Angela Kanady Slay
November 25, 2022

Made in the USA
Columbia, SC
29 April 2025

57293416R00061